Hal Leonard
結他入門 第一輯
Guitar Method • Book 1
by Will Schmid

偉・士文博士（Dr. Will Schmid）是暢銷的 Hal Leonard Guitar Method 及另外40多件包括盒帶，鐳射唱碟和錄影帶的結他和班卓琴教材的作者。士文博士除了任職美國威斯康新大學結他課程主席外，更替 Hal Leonard 出版的多部音樂教材從事編輯工作。

Translated by: David Cheng

翻譯：鄭永健

目 錄

HAL•LEONARD® CORPORATION
7777 W. BLUEMOUND RD. P.O. BOX 13819 MILWAUKEE, WI 53213

前 言

當這部結他教材在1997年初版時，我跟多位結他老師談論過他們對這部教材的觀感和意見。他們的意見對改良這部教材有莫大的幫助。為了更加改良這部教材(Book1)，我也向其他多位著名的結他老師們發出問卷，他們對這部教材也提供很多寶貴的建議。我在歸納各方的資料並作出改良以後，這部教材(Hal Leonand Guitar Method)受到眾多結他老師和學生的支持，並已翻譯成超過八種語言在世界各地發行。

Will Schmid

現特別鳴謝：Kirk Likes

你 的 結 他

這部教材的內容適用於任何結他 - 電結他，鋼線，尼龍線的木結他等。而這些結他亦可彈奏各類型的音樂。

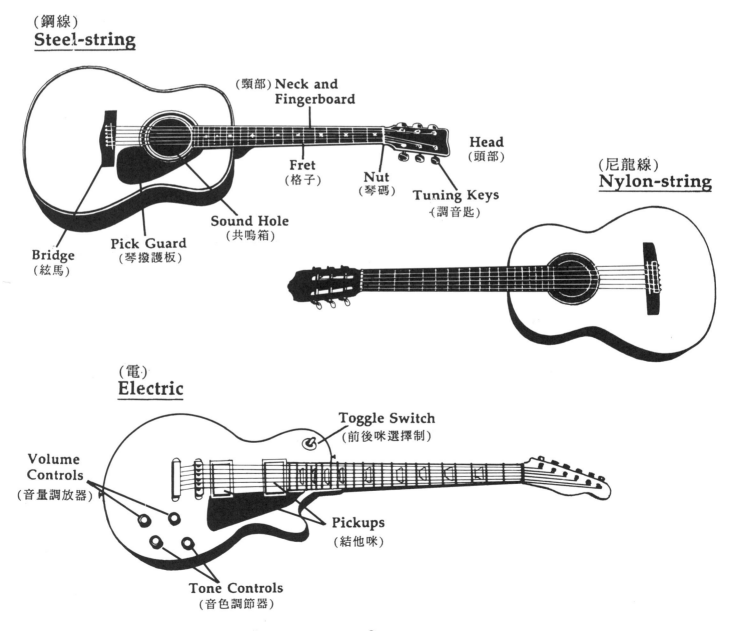

（鋼線）
Steel-string

（頸部）**Neck and Fingerboard**

Head
（頭部）

（尼龍線）
Nylon-string

Fret
（格子）

Nut
（琴碼）

Tuning Keys
（調音匙）

Sound Hole
（共鳴箱）

Pick Guard
（琴撥護板）

Bridge
（絃馬）

（電）
Electric

Toggle Switch
（前後咪選擇制）

Volume Controls
（音量調放器）

Pickups
（結他咪）

Tone Controls
（音色調節器）

調 音 ① （鐳射碟的歌目編號）

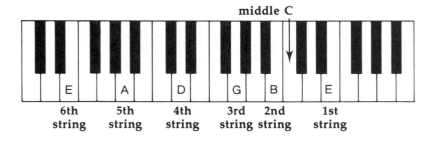

當你調較結他弦的音度時，你需要調整結他上的調音匙(Tuning Keys)。以收緊或放鬆弦線。若把結他弦收緊，就即是把弦的音度調高，放鬆就是調低。

我們把結他弦編為1-6弦，數目是小的就是最幼的弦線，也是貼近你的膝部，如此類推。我們順次序由第6弦開始調較，若各位利用鋼琴作為調聲的標準工具(附圖)，請耐心地調整調音匙直至每條弦發出的音度和鋼琴發出相同的音度一致為止。

TUNING KEYS (調音匙)

1—E
2—B
3—G
4—D
5—A
6—E

利用結他調音器 (Electronic Guitar Tuner)

結他調音器可閱讀結他弦的音度是否準確，而調音器是一個十分可靠的調音工具。市面上有多種的結他調音器發售，而每種都有不同的設計和使用方法．

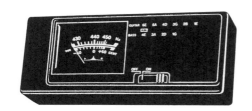

Keyboard (琴鍵)

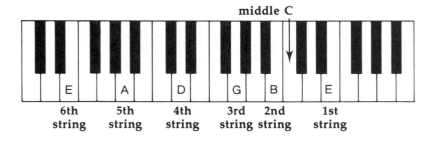

middle C

E	A	D	G	B	E
6th string	5th string	4th string	3rd string	2nd string	1st string

調音的其他方法 （相關調音）

當你在沒有調音器和其他樂器提供調音標準的時候，請試用以下方法：

• 假定結他上的第6弦是準確地調至E音。

• 按下第6弦的第5格，第5格正發出A音，而A音正是第5弦該調至的音度。利用你的姆指同時撥第5弦和按下第5格的6弦，當2弦發出的聲調一致時，該弦的調音已完成。

• 按下第5弦的第5格，調整第4弦直至2弦音度相同。（跟調較第5，6弦的程序一樣）

• 按下第4弦的第5格，調整第3弦。

• 當調整第2弦時，則要按下第3弦的第4格。

• 按下第2弦的第5格，調整第1弦。

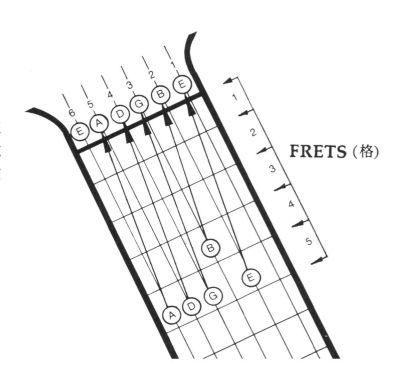

FRETS (格)

彈結他的姿勢

有幾個自然舒適的彈結他姿勢提供給各位，圖左是坐著彈結他，圖右則是站著，另外有幾個意見給各位參考來建立正確的演奏姿勢：

- 當彈奏結他的時候，要保持身體各部份，例如：手，腳和身體在一個鬆弛的狀態，盡量避免身體任何音部份有拉緊的感覺。

- 當在演奏的時候，若身體部份感到拉緊的話，你的演奏姿勢可能不正確，要留意及改良自己的姿勢。

- 結他的頸部經常保持微微向上傾斜-切勿向下傾。

- 保持結他的身體垂直，切勿把結他的身體向前傾，這樣對你的留意自己的彈奏手法其實沒有幫助。保持結他平衡，並保持腰部挺直，更重要是保持身體鬆弛。

留意我替手指編上號碼1-4，當拿著結他頸部的時候，把拇指放在結他頸部的後面，留意右圖，當拿住結他的時候，拇指和中指前後平排在結他頸上，而手掌部份該微微離開結他頸的背部，切勿緊抓結他的頸部。（請看附圖）

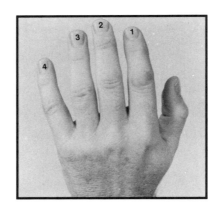 

左圖顯示拿 "琴撥" (PICK)的姿勢，而圖二顯示右手拿著琴撥並準備演奏時的姿勢。留意手指在演奏時要保持輕鬆和靈活。

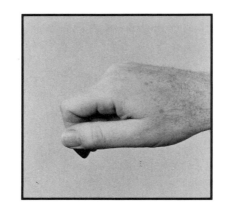 

音 樂 符 號

記錄音樂的方式是把音樂化作符號，記錄在譜表(STAFF) 之上。譜表是由五條線組成，而每條
線和線之間代表不同的音調 (PITCH) 。每份樂譜之前端都會有一個譜號 (CLEF SIGN) 。我們
常用高音譜號來記錄結他音樂。

每條線和線之間代表 1 個調音: 線 (LINES)(由最底至頂) ， E-G-B-D-F (一個有趣的方法以使
便記憶(Every Guitarist Begins Doing Fine) ：線與線之間 (由最底至頂) ，F-A-C-E，可以拼出一
個英文字 "FACE"

譜表是由多個小節組成 (MEASURE)，而小節與小節之間是用小節線分開 (BAR LINES) 。每
段樂章的結尾部份都會劃上雙小節線 (DOUBLE BAR LINE) 。

每個小節內有一組節拍。節拍是音樂的骨幹，把音樂有規律地表達出來。

音符(NOTES) 代表每個調音的長度。

不同的音符放在譜表的線或線與線之間的位置可以表達出音符的長度和調音。

第1弦上的音調

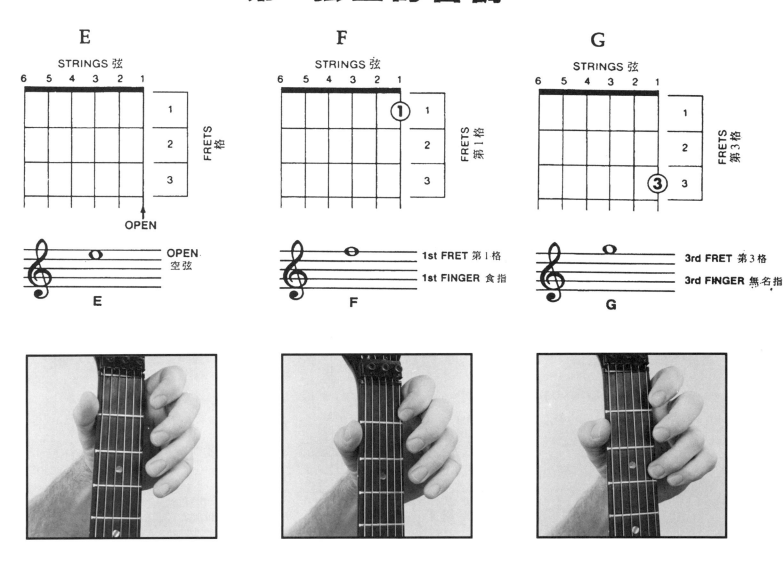

（∏）代表利用琴撥向下彈弦線

當你剛剛開始練習這些練習曲時，請從一個較慢的彈奏速度開始，當你能夠掌握這此練習精華後，再續漸把彈奏的速度增快。

請用指尖的部份按弦。

請保持左手微微的拱起。

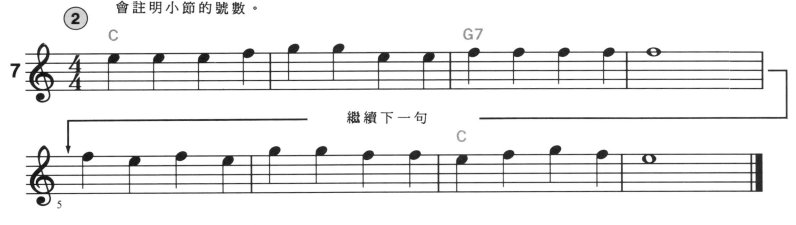

以下的練習曲比較長，請你連續彈奏第1和2句音樂(切勿在彈奏第一句後停止，然後才彈第2句)。灰色的字代表老師將會彈奏的和弦。每句練習曲的開始都會註明小節的號數。

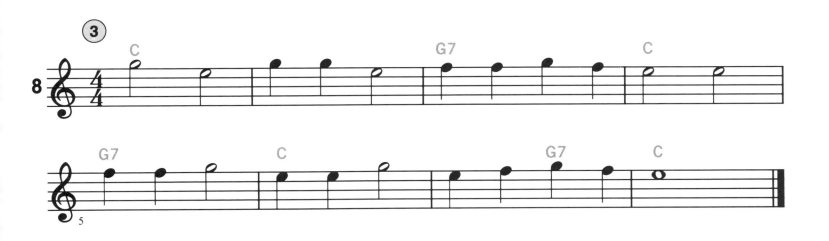

繼續下一句

7

第2弦上的音調

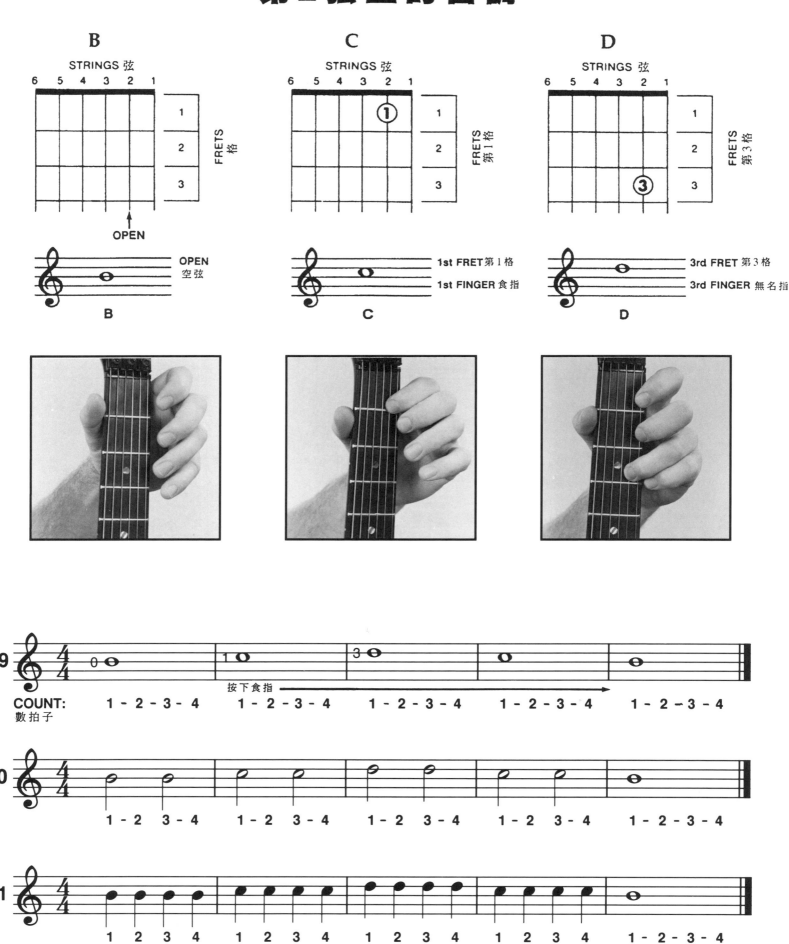

當你練習這些練習曲的時候，請用一個較慢的彈奏速度練習，並要留意拍子是否穩定。當你對練習曲有一定的掌握之後，才把練習曲的彈奏速度加快。若你在練習的時候，發覺奏出的聲音"不乾淨"，請留意你的左手的手指，耐心地練習，直至奏出"乾淨"的聲音為止。

過線練習

在剛才的練習，你已學會了第1弦和2弦的第1至3格。在以下的練習曲，你將會需要彈奏結他上的第1和2弦。當你在"過線"之前，先留意手指要按的位置，然後準確地按。

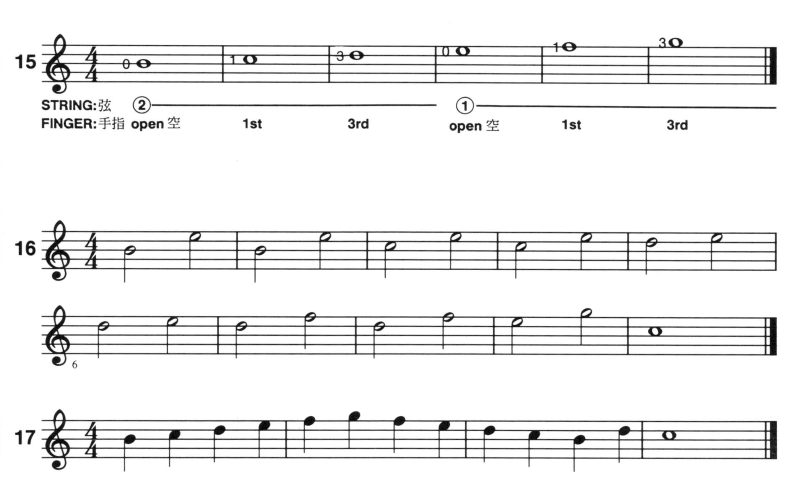

以下的練習曲需要用第1及2弦去彈奏。經常在初開始時用一個慢的彈奏速度，
在熟習後， 才加快彈速。灰色的和弦符號將由導師替你奏出。

ODE TO JOY ④ ⑤

Beethoven

以下是一首需要1-3人合奏的練習曲。當第1位奏者，彈至(＊)號位置的時候，下
一位奏者便可加入彈奏(由練習曲的頭開始)。當第2位彈至(＊)號位置時，第3位
也加入，而每位奏者需把整首練習曲彈奏2次。

ROUND ⑥

第 3 線 的 音 調

G   A

經常保持手指(按格的一邊手)微微彎曲,使手指有充裕時間準備按下一個音。

以下的練習曲，需要利用結他的第1至3弦彈奏。

準確是練習彈奏結他的首要注意，在（練習曲）掌握到後才把彈速加快
些。（練習曲亦可作為手指熱身練習。）

YANKEE DOODLE

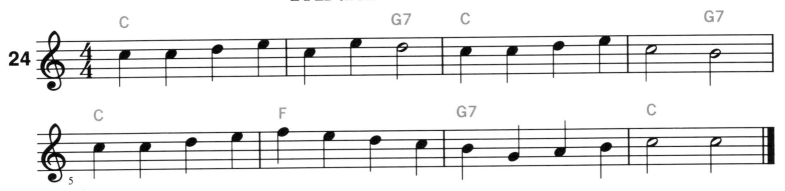

以下的雙重奏曲，由2個部份組成。請把2個部份都充份練習，你可找導師或朋
友跟你一起彈奏。或者，你可先把其中1個部份彈奏及錄起，然後把錄好的部份
播出，並練習同時彈奏第2部。當你掌握得到雙重奏後，把選擇獨奏句加上。

THE BELLS

AU CLAIR DE LA LUNE ⑦

France

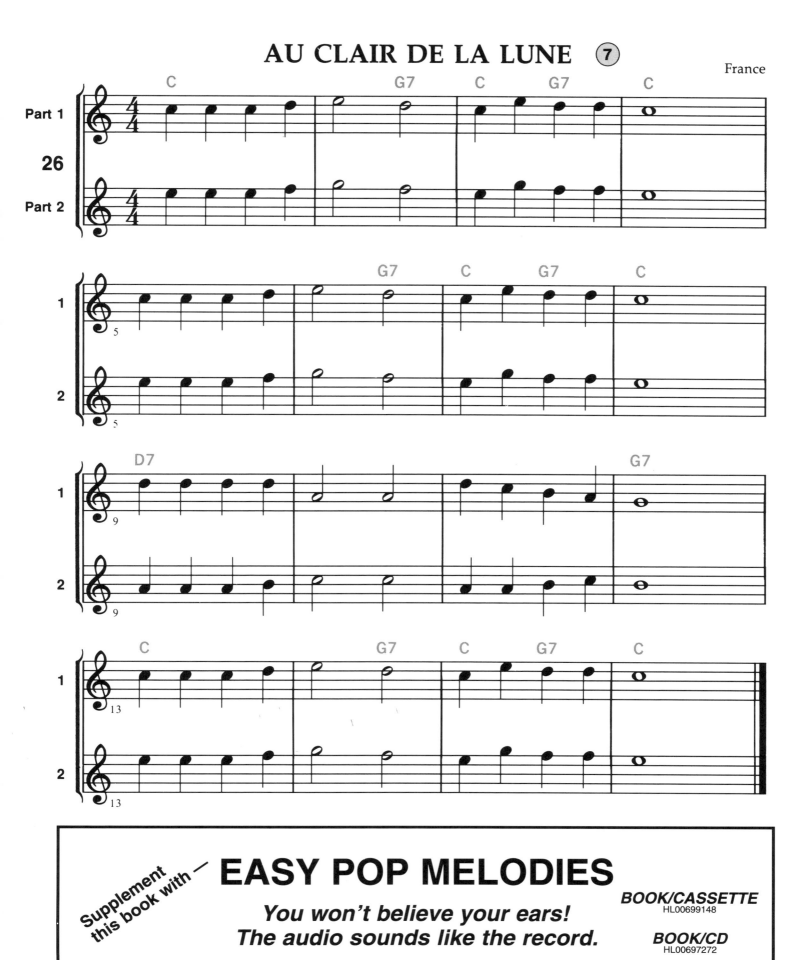

AURA LEE

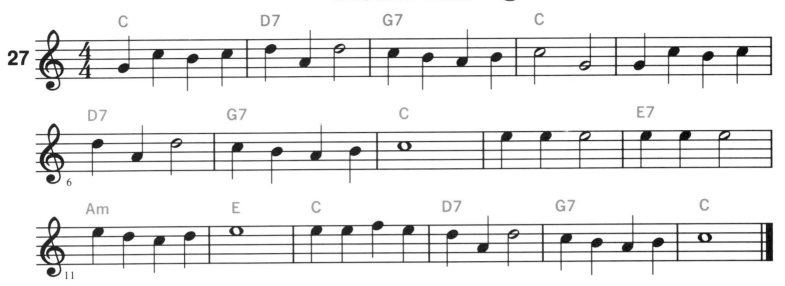

有些音樂每個小節只有3拍。每首歌的前面的拍
號上面的號數會指示出，而下面的數字（4）代表
每一個4分音符代表1拍。

音符後的點代表把音符的總值加1半。
$\frac{3}{4}$ 拍號裡即是3拍

每個小節3拍

4分音(♩)符為1拍

$\frac{3}{4}$ ♩ + • = ♩·
2拍　　1拍　　3拍

COUNT:　1　2　3　1 - 2　3　1　2　3　1 - 2 - 3　1　2 - 3　1 - 2 - 3
拍子

HE'S A JOLLY GOOD FELLOW ⑨

England

14

3弦 → 和弦

當多過1個音一起奏出，我們稱之為"和弦"。我們先學一些只需按下一個音的和弦。

我們由第1弦撥下去(2弦和1弦)。請留意3條弦應一同發聲。

C Chord

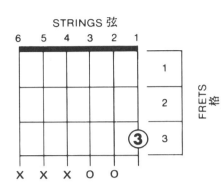

G Chord

G7 Chord

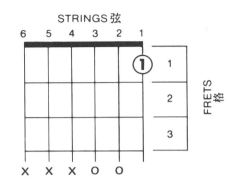

o = 空弦
x = 不用彈

請保持彈奏時拍子要保持穩定。

更多的和弦指法，請參考P.47

結他獨奏

在以前的練習，各位已分別練習過彈奏旋律及和弦，這個練習曲將會把旋律和和弦串連起來。請先練習彈奏旋律，然後練習彈奏和弦，最後把2部份串起來。請由慢的彈速開始練習，然後漸漸加快。

MARIANNE ⑩

Caribbean

All day, all night Mar - i - anne,

Down by the sea - side sift - in' sand.

E - ven lit - tle chil - dren love Mar - i - anne,

Down by the sea - side sift - in' sand.

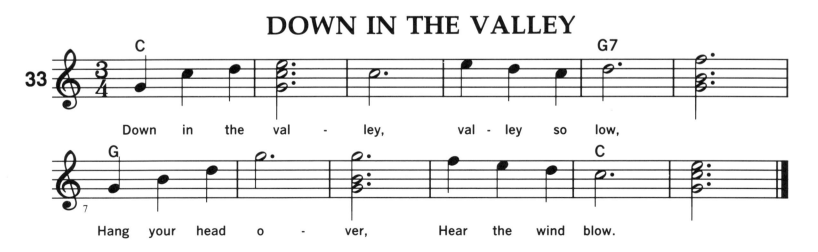

DOWN IN THE VALLEY

Down in the val - ley, val - ley so low,

Hang your head o - ver, Hear the wind blow.

第 4 線 的 音 調

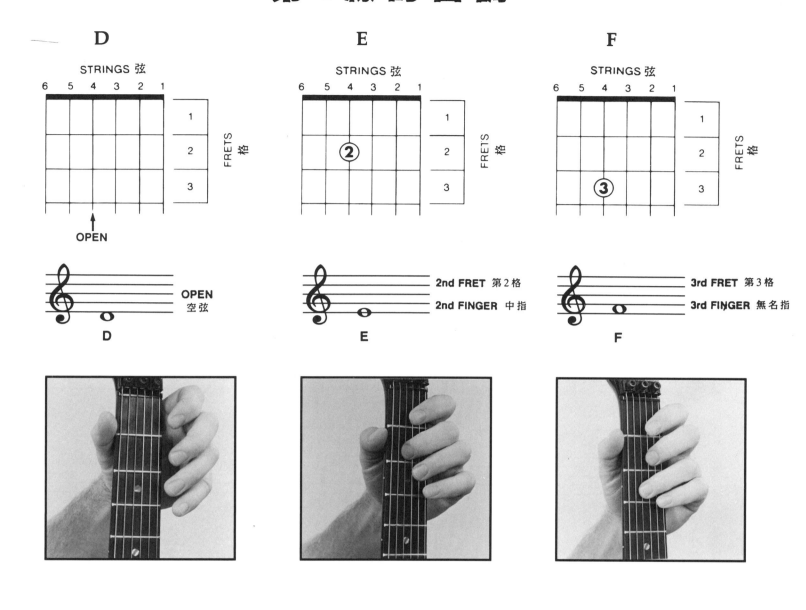

D   **E**   **F**

STRINGS 弦   STRINGS 弦   STRINGS 弦

OPEN   2nd FRET 第2格 / 2nd FINGER 中指   3rd FRET 第3格 / 3rd FINGER 無名指

OPEN 空弦

D   **E**   **F**

請留意保持手指微微彎曲

34

1 - 2   3 - 4   Hold 2nd finger down. ⟶

35

17

Pickup Notes

有很大部份的歌曲並不是從第1個小節的第1拍開始。在第一個小節前的音，稱之為（Pick up notes）。以下是一些（Pick up notes）的例子。當你彈奏有（Pick up notes）的旋律時，請把整個小節也加進旋律之前，先數節拍，再開始彈奏(如圖)

THE RIDDLE SONG ⑪ ⑫

當旋律的前邊有Pick up notes，旋律的尾（最後一個小節）也會欠缺一些拍子（與Pick up notes的拍數相同）

你可邀請一位朋友，老師，甚至錄下彈奏和弦部份來練習。

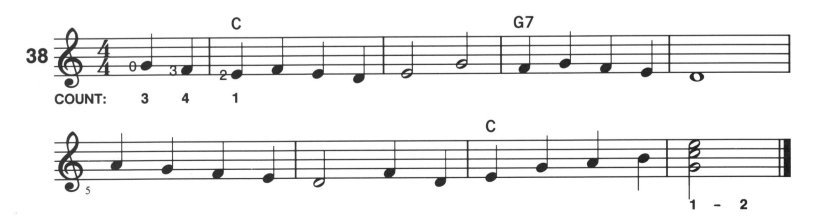

D7 和弦

D7和弦在指板上排成剛好一個三角形，相信對很多朋友來說，都很容易掌握。請用指尖部份按線，並由第4弦撥下去。

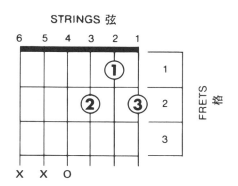

每個斜線代表撥和弦1 次。

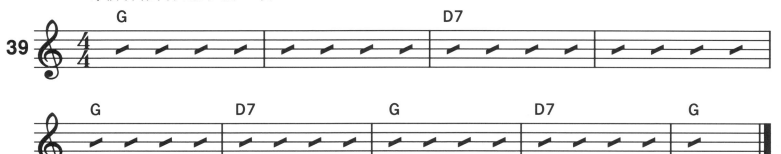

請重溫C和弦的指法，並重覆3練習 練習曲40，並保持在轉彈C和D7和弦時，食指盡量貼近指板。

12-BAR BLUES-ROCK ⑬ ⑭

請邀請你的導師和朋友參與一起練習。

WORRIED MAN BLUES ⑮ ⑯

42

I takes a wor-ried man to sing a wor-ried song, It
takes a wor-ried man to sing a wor-ried song, It
takes a wor-ried man to sing a wor-ried song, I'm wor-ried
now, yes now, but I won't be wor-ried long.

連線

一條曲線把2個相同的音符連起，我們稱之為 "連線"。
連線把2個音符的值都加起來，請留意下面連線的例子。

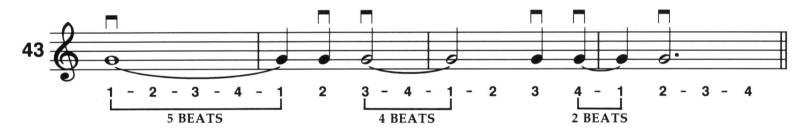

43

1 - 2 - 3 - 4 - 1   2   3 - 4 - 1 - 2   3   4 - 1   2 - 3 - 4
5 BEATS   **4 BEATS**   **2 BEATS**

AMAZING GRACE ⑰

44

A - maz - ing Grace, How sweet the sound, That
saved a wretch like me; _____ I once was lost, but
1 - 2 - 3 - 1 - 2
now am found; Was blind, but now I see. _____
1 - 2 - 3 - 1 - 2

WHEN THE SAINTS GO MARCHING IN ⑱ ⑲

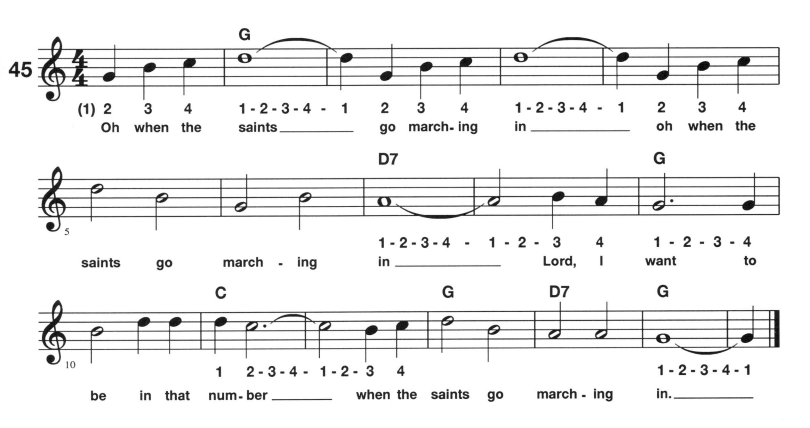

你可邀請你的導師或朋友為你彈奏練習曲的和弦部份（灰色字），而你則要負責彈奏旋律部份。

THE GYPSY GUITAR

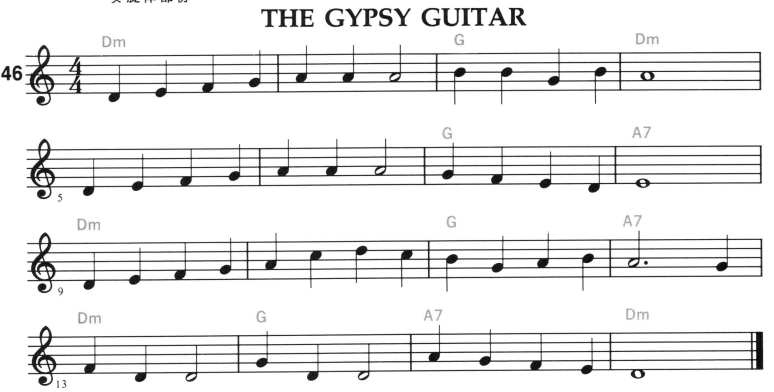

第 5 線 的 音 調

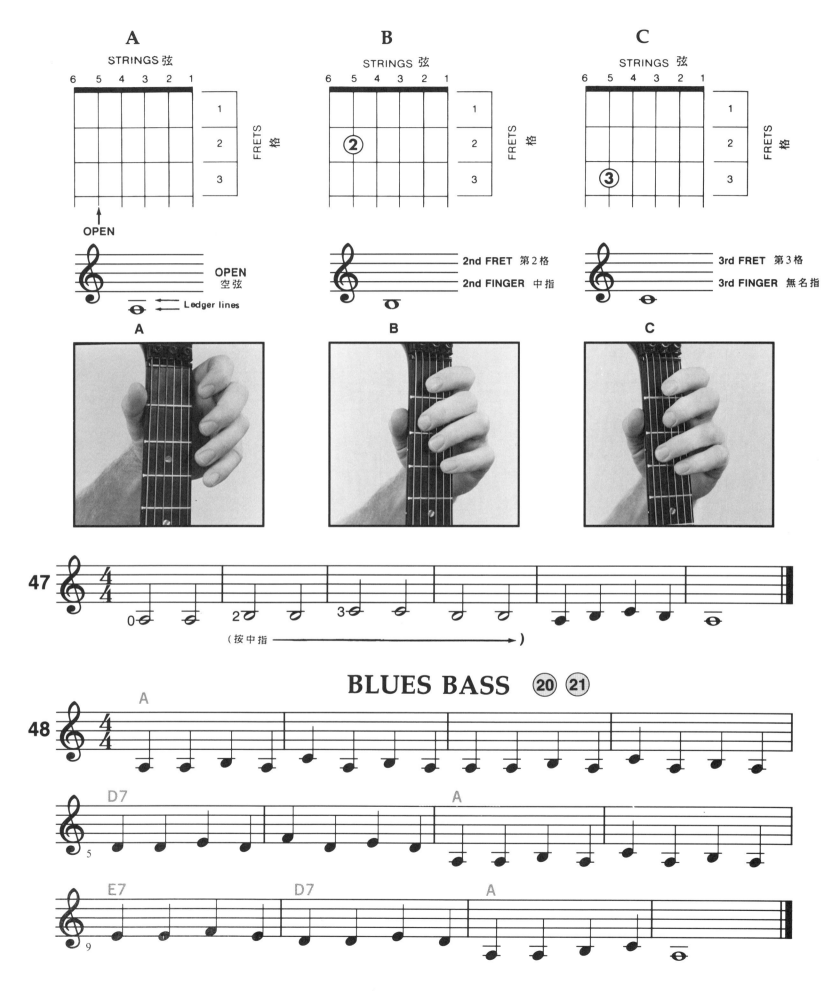

請練習以下2首練習曲的旋律部份，並留意你的精神應集中於比你正在彈奏的部份更前（將要彈奏的部份）的部份，換句話說，你的精神應預覽將要彈的部份。

THE VOLGA BOATMAN

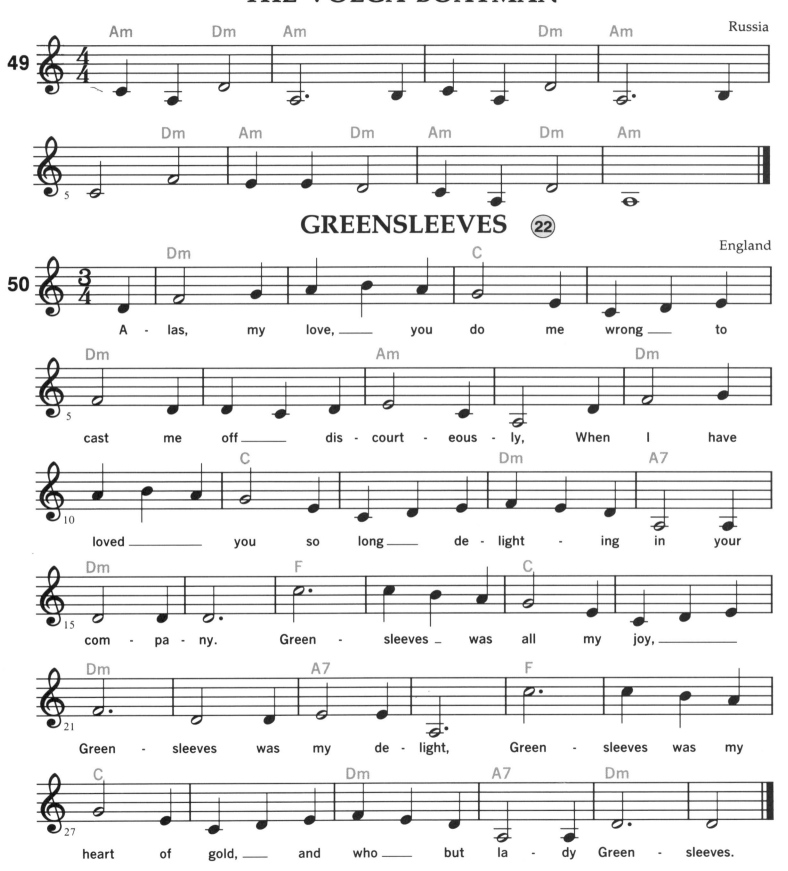

GREENSLEEVES

A - las, my love, ____ you do me wrong ____ to
cast me off ____ dis - court - eous - ly, When I have
loved ____ you so long ____ de - light - ing in your
com - pa - ny. Green - sleeves _ was all my joy, ____
Green - sleeves was my de - light, Green - sleeves was my
heart of gold, ____ and who ____ but la - dy Green - sleeves.

第 5 線 的 音 調

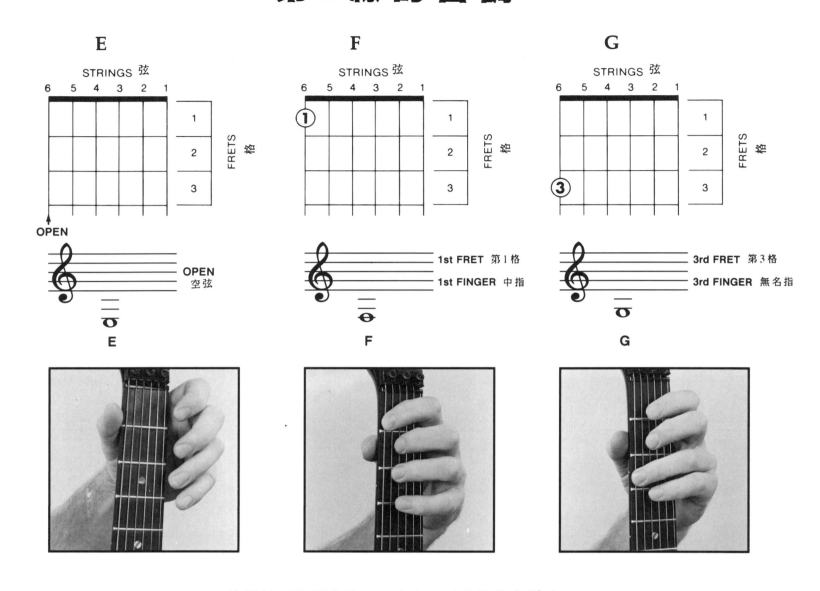

E   F   G

OPEN 空弦 — E

1st FRET 第1格 — 1st FINGER 中指 — F

3rd FRET 第3格 — 3rd FINGER 無名指 — G

練習以下練習曲後，請寫出以下音符的名稱。

51

用1st指按下 ———————————————————→

52

53

JOHNNY HAS GONE FOR A SOLDIER ㉓

Ireland

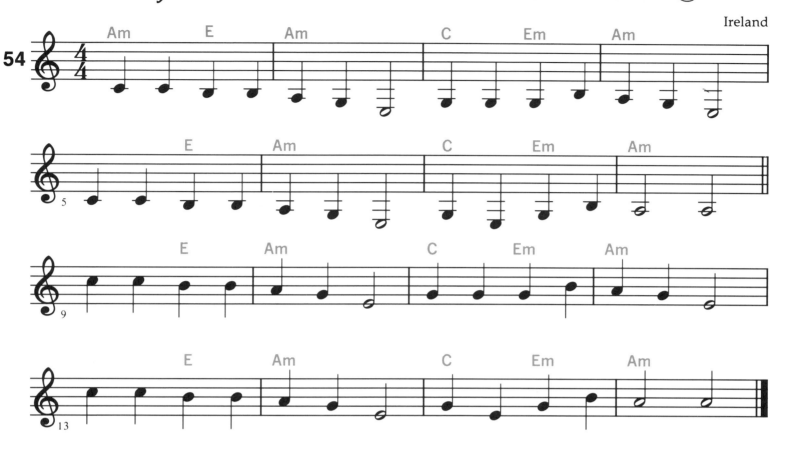

2個音調相同，但相距8度的度的音程，叫做8度音(Octave)。練習曲Johnny
has gone for a Soldier的第2部份，跟第1部份的旋律相同，但高一個8度。

Octaves

BASS ROCK

* Power chords (no 3rd) may be used throughout.

度與半度

音調和音調之間的距離，我們用2個單位來量度－1度和半度。在結他頸上，1格的距離為之半度，2格的距離為之1度(任何方向)。

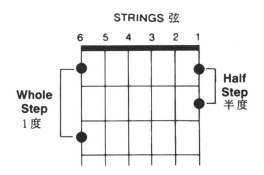

F-Sharp(F#)升音階

當升音階 (#) 出現於音符的左邊時，代表該音調升高半度 (結他頸上即升高1格)。升音階亦代表隨了該音調外，該小節內的相同的音調亦會被升高。

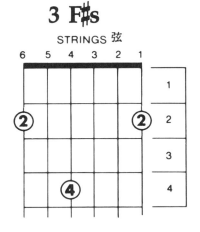

3 F#s

1st string 弦	4th string 弦	6th string 弦
2nd fret 格	4th fret 格	2nd fret 格

請重覆練習以下練習曲。

LONDONDERRY AIR ㉔

Ireland

音調符號 (Key Signatures)

為避免在閱譜的時候出現混亂，(舉例：F#)一個升音階 (#) 將會出現於樂譜開始的F線上。這個正是所謂的調號 (Key Signature)，亦代表該歌曲內的F該當作為F#。在練習曲Shenandoah中，箭咀所指示的正是提醒你們把F當作F#彈奏

練習曲Shenandoah是首可供2-3人合奏的作品。當彈奏第1部份(旋律)時，請注意連線部份的拍子，請耐心地把拍子準確地彈奏(或可借助拍子機)。你也可找來另外2位朋友負責彈奏第2部份和和弦部份來合奏此曲。

SHENANDOAH ㉕

Sea Shanty

休止符 (Rests)

休止符代表安靜。休止符也有多種的類別，而不同的類別代表安靜的時間長短。

Whole（全休止符）　　　　**Half**（二分休止符）　　　　**Quarter**（四分休止符）

靜四拍　　　　　　　　　　靜二拍　　　　　　　　　　靜一拍

當你遇上休止符的時候，你需要停止結他發出任何聲音。
一個常用的方法是利用右手的手掌側部按在弦線上（如圖）。
若需要的話，請重覆練習，用最少的手部動作達至靜止的
效果為最佳。

當練習彈奏以下練習曲時，請朗聲數出所有的拍子，若遇
上休止符，請朗出 "靜"（如：數拍的指示）

COUNT:　1　2　3　Rest　1　Rest　3　Rest　Rest　2　3　4　1 - 2　Rest　Rest
　　　　　　　　　　　靜　　　　靜　　　　靜　靜

R 代表休止符

1　2　R　R　　R　2　3　4　　R　R　R　R　　1　R　3　4　　1 - 2 - 3　R

1　R　R　4　1 - 2　R　R　1　2　3 - 4　1　R　R　R

在 3/4 的樂曲中，全音符的休止符 (▬) 代表一個小節 3 拍休止符

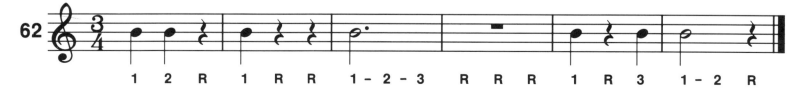

1　2　R　1　R　R　1 - 2 - 3　R　R　R　1　R　3　1 - 2　R

ROCK 'N' REST ㉖

Count rests aloud: 請 郎 出 靜

JACK STUART ㉗

Scottish

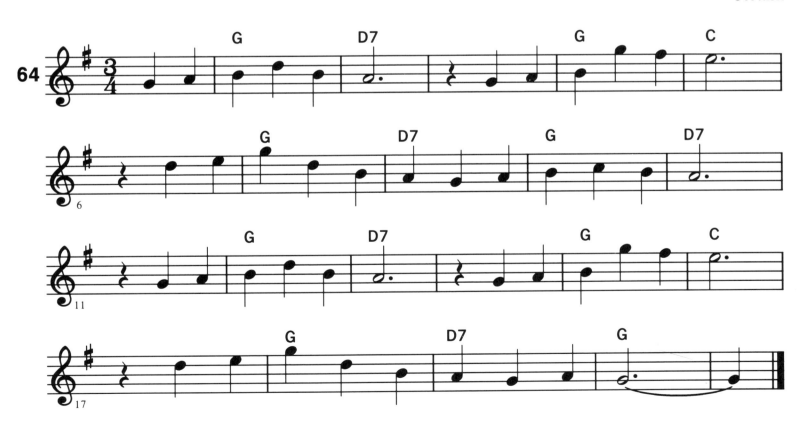

C, G, G7 和弦

在本書前部份，向各位介紹過一些只用3條弦彈奏出的C和G7和弦。在本節會介紹一些利用第5-6條弦奏出的C和G7和弦，而這些和弦所奏出的聲音會比較豐富。請跟下圖的指示，並重覆練習。

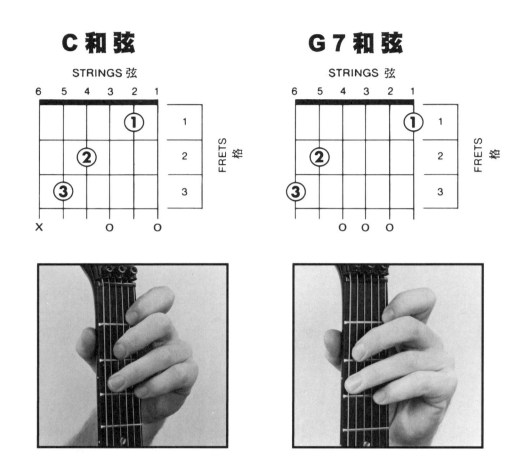

C 和弦 / G 7 和弦

此 :|| 符號叫作 "重覆記號"，代表重覆剛才彈奏的音樂多一遍。

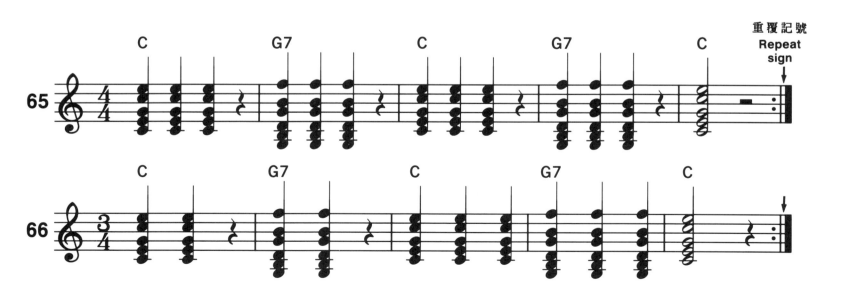

以下是其他2個G和弦的不同"指法"。請留意2個和弦的不同指法,左圖2,3,4的指法比較難掌握,但這個指法會在G和弦轉至C和弦時較為含接。若你的手指較短的話,可先學習123指法的G和弦。

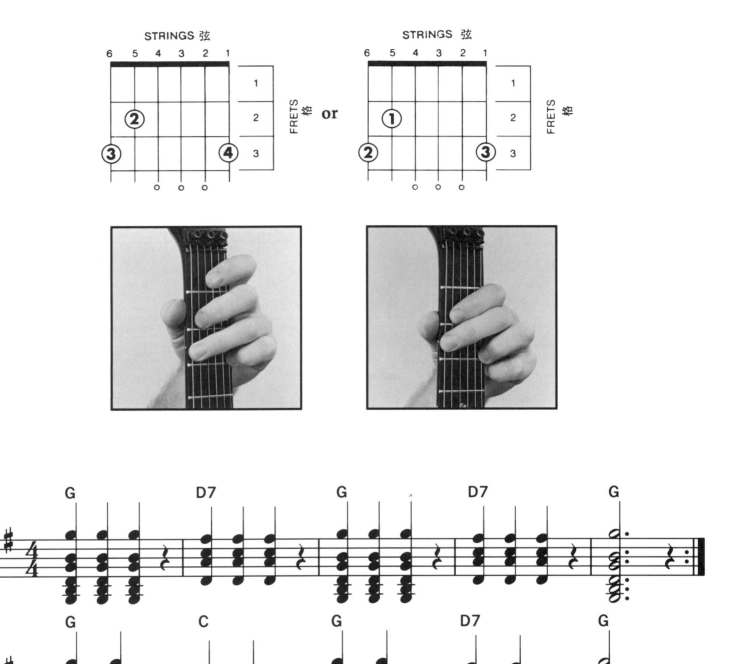

當熟習了練習67及68的練習後,請以strummed chord代替休止符。

請把以下練習曲的旋律和和弦部份輪流練習。

WILL THE CIRCLE BE UNBROKEN

Country gospel

Will the cir - cle _____ be un - bro - ken, _____ by and
by, Lord, by and by? There's a
bet - ter _____ home a - wait - ing, _____ in the
sky, Lord, _____ in the _____ sky. _____

CORINNA

Blues

Oh, oh, Cor - in - na where you been so long?
Oh, oh, Cor - in - na where you been so long?
Ain't had no lov - in' since you been gone.

IRISH TUNE (30)

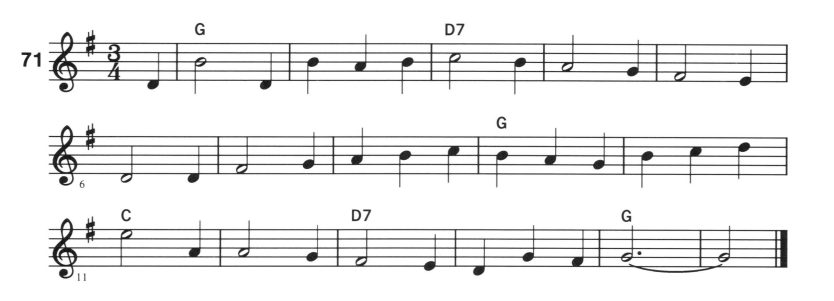

低音 / 撥弦

在撥弦之前，先彈奏所屬和弦的低音（例如：G和弦，G為低音）。你可以自由組合出不同的低音和撥弦組合（如：練習72）。

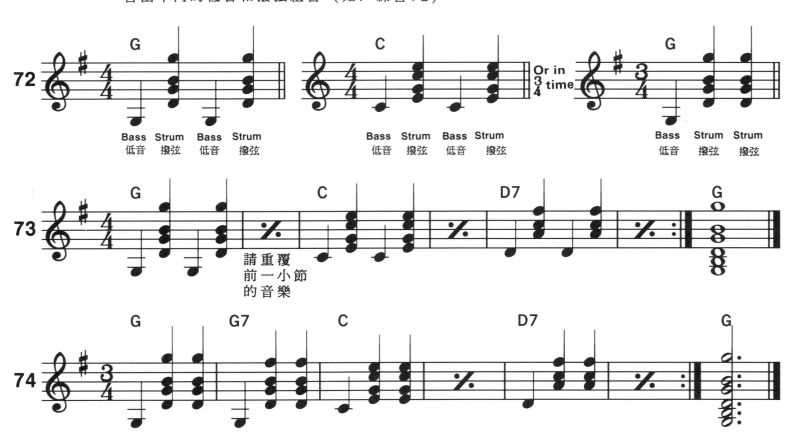

當你充份掌握這個低音/撥弦的練習後，請把這個練習應用於本書其他練習曲中。

8分音符

8分音符的長度是4分音符的1半，（無論在 4/4 或 3/4） 亦即是半拍。

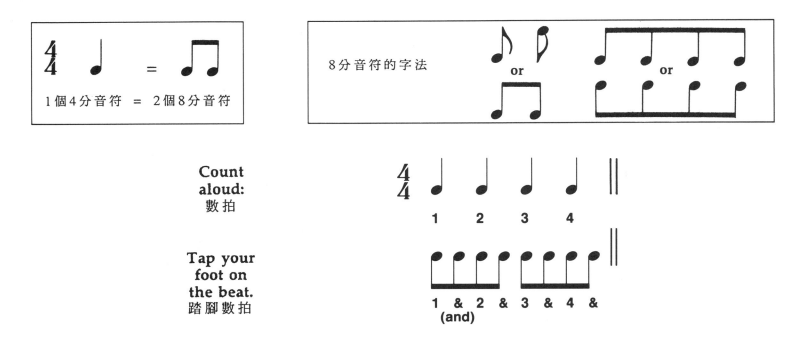

以下8分音符上的(П)代表向下撥弦，而(V)則代表向上撥弦。

請跟隨練習曲76上的符號指示，當彈奏8分音符時，用向上及下撥弦，而4分音符則只須向下撥弦。請留意踏腳數拍和撥弦兩個動作的關係，當腳下踏時，手向下撥，當腳踏向上時，手向上撥弦。

請用較慢的速度練習，當充分掌握練習後，才把速度續漸加快。

TIRED SAILOR (31)

Sea Shanty

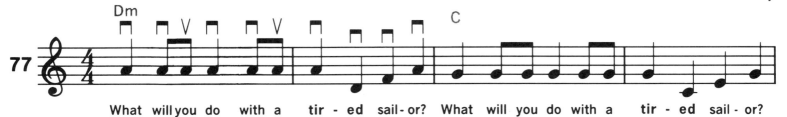

What will you do with a tir-ed sail-or? What will you do with a tir-ed sail-or?

What will you do with a tir-ed sail-or, ear-ly in the morn-ing?

FRERE JACQUES

France

Frè-re Jac-ques, frè-re Jac-ques, Dor-mez vous? dor-mez vous?
Are you sleep-ing? Are you sleep-ing? Broth-er John, Broth-er John,

Son-nez les ma-tin-es, son-nez les ma-tin-es, Din, din, don; din, din, don.
Morn-ing bells are ring-ing, Morn-ing bells are ring-ing, ding, dong, ding; ding,dong,ding.

Frere Jacques 是一首可由多人參與的練習曲，當第1個參與者奏至星號（＊）時，第2位參與者可開始加入（從練習曲的開端開始彈奏）。

SAILORS HORNPIPE

請在開始彈奏之前，先留意每首歌的調號。Boogie BASS 的 F 是 F#

BOOGIE BASS ③② ③③

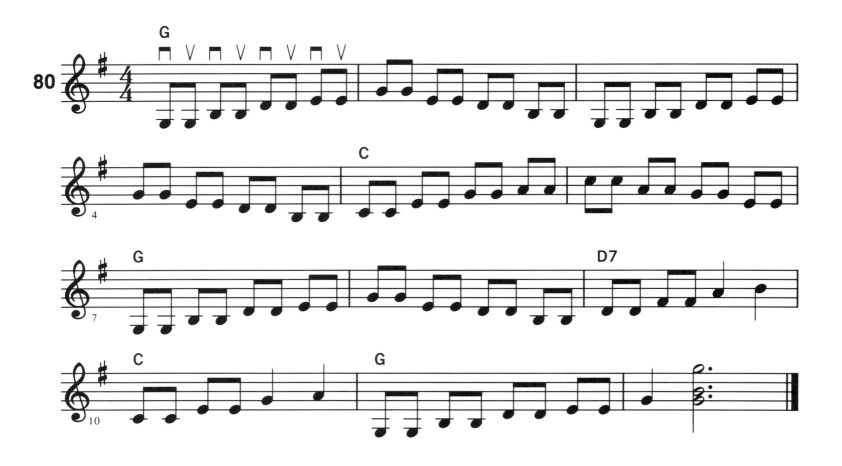

3-PART ROUND

E 小調和弦

Em

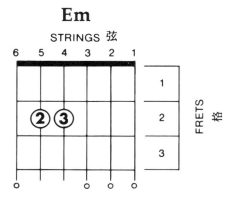

在本書較前的章節中介紹過和弦的不同指法，而 E 小調和弦也有不同的指法。以下的例子列出 E 小調和弦不同的指法。（左為較完整及聲音較豐富的指法，右圖為較簡單的指法）

當你彈奏 E 小調和弦的時候，你可利用 E 弦（第 6 弦）作低音，而加上較簡單的指法（如圖），做出較前章節介紹的低音／撥弦的彈奏手法。

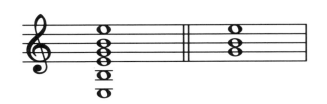

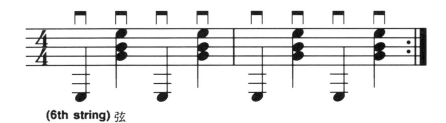

(6th string) 弦

HEY, HO, NOBODY HOME

England

82

Em

Hey, ho, no - bod - y home, Meat, nor drink, nor mon - ey have I none, Yet will I be mer - - - - ry

SHALOM CHAVERIM

Israel

83

Em
*

Sha - lom, cha - ve - rim! Sha - lom, cha - ve - rim! Sha - lom, sha - lom! Le - hit - ra - ot, le - hit - ra - ot, Sha - lom, sha - lom.

*用輪唱歌曲來演奏

37

當你彈奏不同和弦的時候，請留意不同和弦之間有沒有音調相同。當你發現（例如：G和Em和弦及C和D7和弦）2個和弦之間有相同音調之時，請在轉換指法之時，保持同音調的手指按著音調。請練習以下練習曲的轉和弦時的指法，直至你能順暢地轉換和弦的指法。

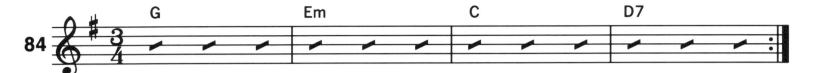

請練習Molly Molone 的旋律及和弦部份，當你能夠掌握彈奏和弦部份時，請把練習74的節奏和低音/撥弦模式用於此練習曲之中。

MOLLY MALONE ㉞

Ireland

複雜的和弦彈奏法

在前章介紹的上下撥弦手法（8分音符）也可用於彈奏和弦。當你練習以下練習時，請保持手腕放鬆和靈活。上下撥弦的手法比你只用向下撥弦手法，更為靈活，而你也要注意上下撥弦手法只需利用手腕部份，切勿運用整條手臂去完成動作。

基本上下撥弦手法

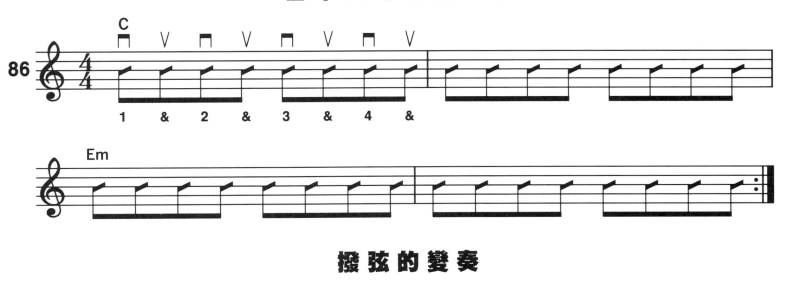

撥弦的變奏

請留意以下練習，在節一拍是減去了一次向上撥弦。

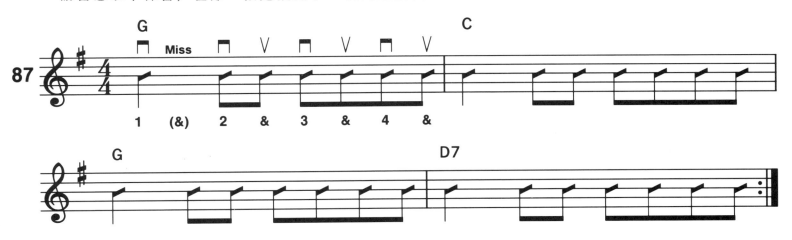

請留意以下練習，在小節內的第1及3拍減去了向上撥弦。

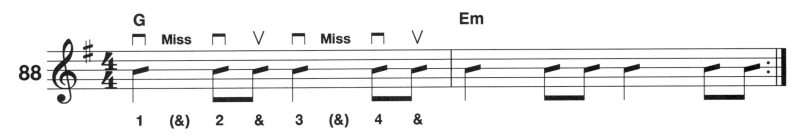

練習曲 "Simple Gift" 共分3個部份　1.)旋律　2.)旋律的和聲　3.)和弦部份

請練習89-90的和弦節奏，並用於Simple Gift的和弦部份。

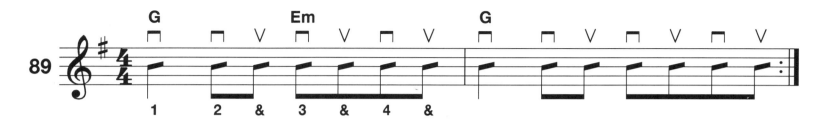

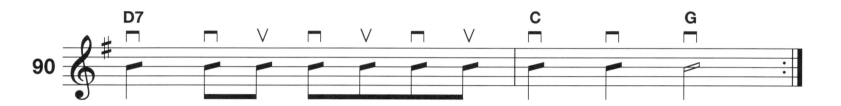

SIMPLE GIFTS 35 36

Shaker song

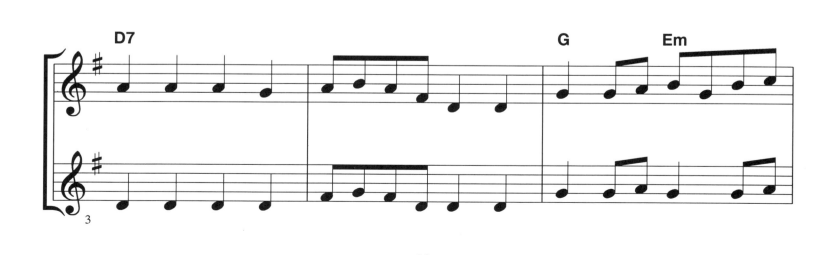

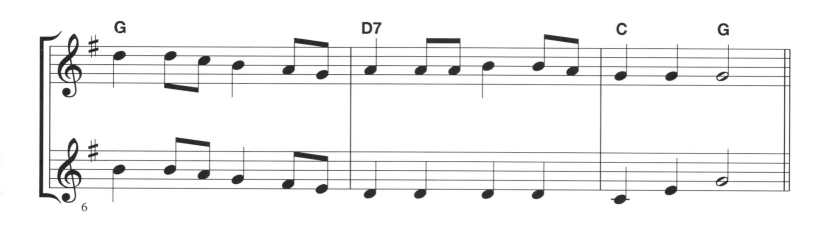

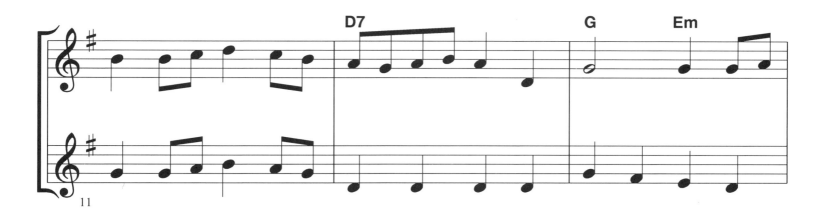

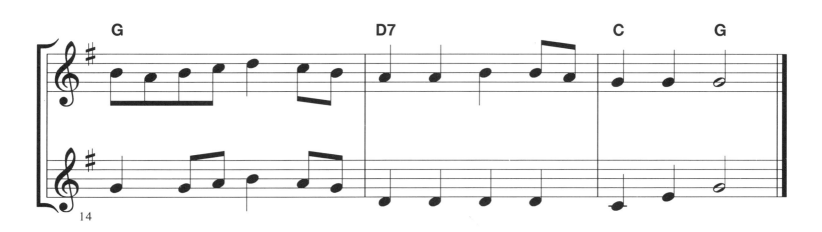

低音-旋律 獨奏

這種獨奏法可於卡特家庭的唱片中找到。旋律部份是利用結他的低音弦彈出,而旋律中間的空位則填滿了撥和弦(如例92)。當你在彈奏時,請強調旋律部份, 而和弦部份則彈得較輕柔。

ROW, ROW, ROW YOUR BOAT

*你在彈奏整首練習曲時,都把第1指(食指) 都下按。

WORRIED MAN BLUES 37 38

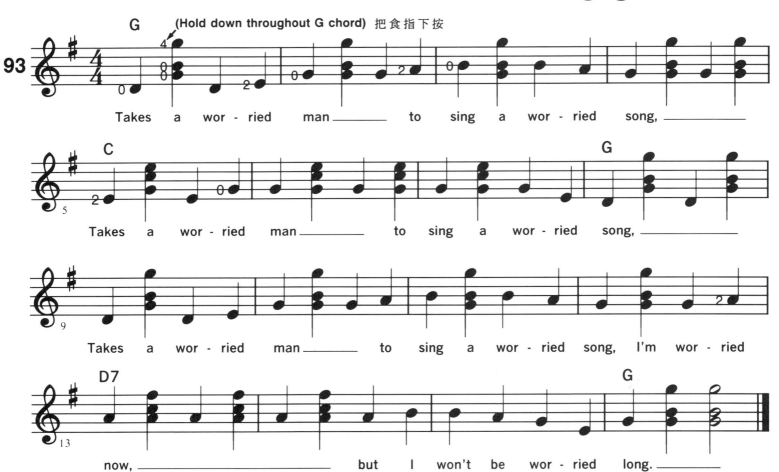

Takes a wor-ried man ____ to sing a wor-ried song, ____

Takes a wor-ried man ____ to sing a wor-ried song, ____

Takes a wor-ried man ____ to sing a wor-ried song, I'm wor-ried

now, ____ but I won't be wor-ried long. ____

WHEN THE SAINTS GO MARCHING IN

Oh when the saints _____ go march-ing in _____ oh when the

saints go march - ing in _____ Lord, I want to

be in that num-ber when the saints go march - ing in.

當你充份掌握這個獨奏手法後，你可改變撥和弦的手法。
把單向下撥(♪)改為(♫)。請重覆練習這個手法。

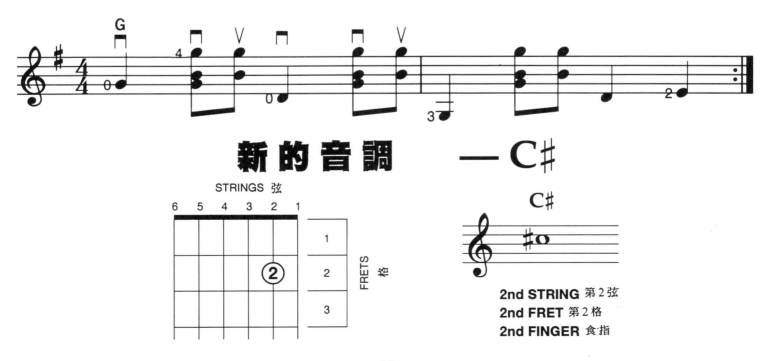

新 的 音 調 — C♯

STRINGS 弦

2nd STRING 第2弦
2nd FRET 第2格
2nd FINGER 食指

MINUET IN G ③⑨ ④⓪

J.S. BACH
*(Guitar 2 arr.
by W. Schmid)*

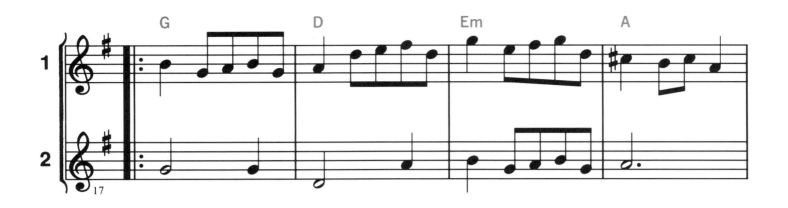

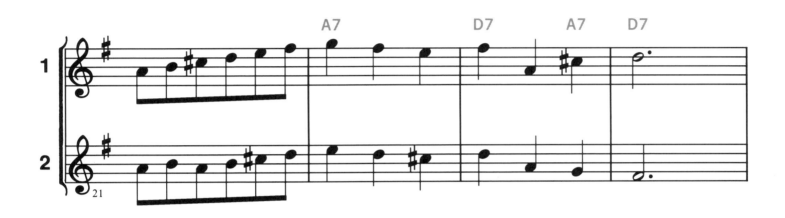

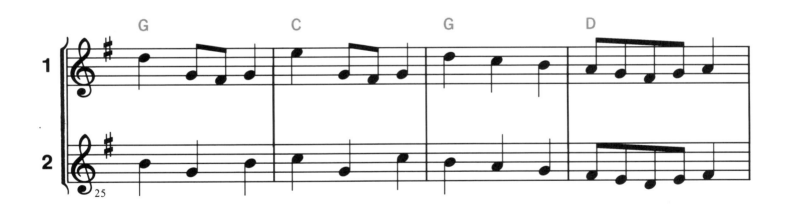

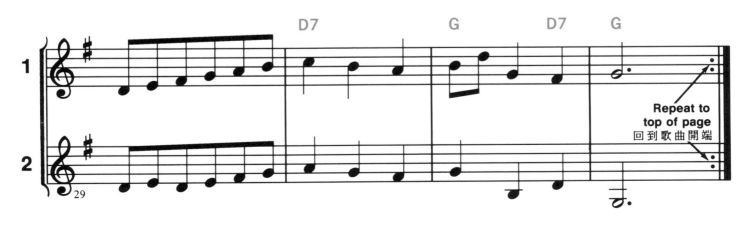

Repeat to top of page
回到歌曲開端

結他合奏

3-part round

以下的合奏曲可以由2-3人合奏。當先彈的一位彈至星號(＊)，另一位則加入(由合奏曲的起源，開始彈奏)，如此類推，而你的老師則可以彈奏和弦部份。請重覆彈奏整首合奏曲3次，並可續漸加快彈速。

和弦表

以下和弦表提供本書有提及過和其他常見和弦的指法。

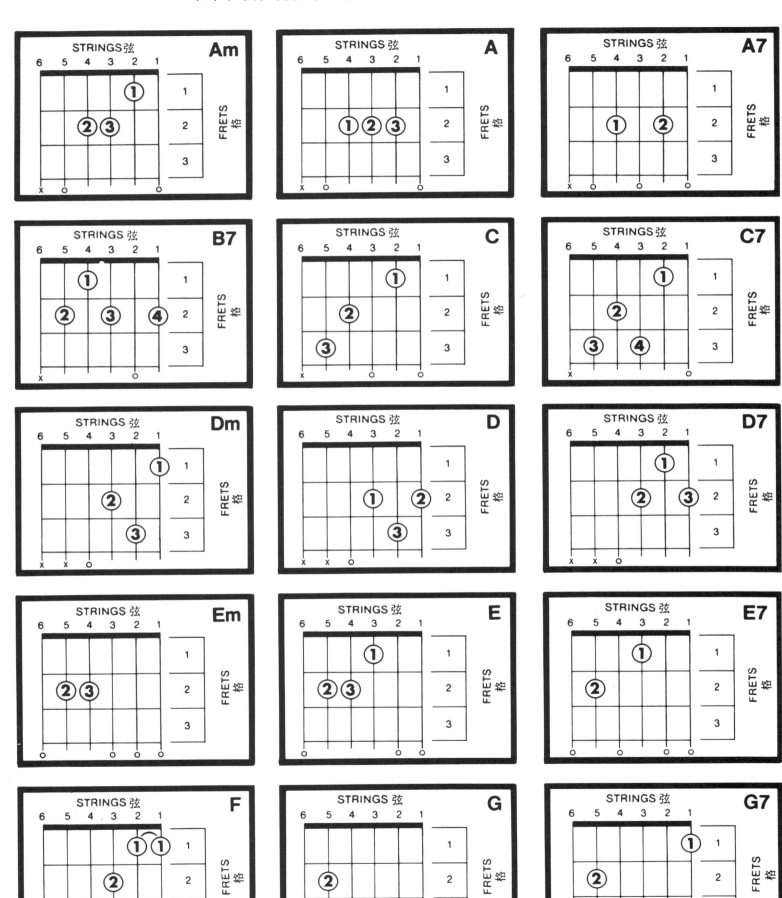

THE HAL LEONARD

GUITAR METHOD

MORE THAN A METHOD ... IT'S A SYSTEM.

This comprehensive method is preferred by teachers and students alike for many reasons:

- Learning sequence is carefully paced with clear instructions that make it easy to learn.
- Popular songs increase the incentive to learn to play.
- Versatile enough to be used as self-instruction or with a teacher.
- Audio accompaniments let students have fun and sound great while practicing.

HAL LEONARD METHOD BOOK 1

Book 1 provides beginning instruction which includes tuning, 1st position melody playing (strings 1-6) the C, G, G7, D7 and Em chords, rhythms through eighth notes, solos and ensembles and strumming. Added features are a chord chart and a selection of traditional songs, including "Amazing Grace," "Greensleeves" and "When the Saints Go Marching In." The optional outstanding recording features audio demos of several exercises with various accompaniments. Tracks include acoustic and electric examples with some played at two different speeds.
00699010 Book $5.95
00699026 Book/Cassette Pack $7.95
00699027 Book/CD Pack..$9.95

HAL LEONARD METHOD BOOK 2

Book 2 includes studies and songs in the keys of C, G, D, Em, and F, syncopations and dotted rhythms, more advanced strums, the most common 1st position chords, solos, bass runs and a variety of styles from bluegrass to blues-rock. A great selection of traditional songs including: "Simple Gifts," "Mamma Don't 'Low," "Roll in My Sweet Baby's Arms," "Jesu, Joy Of Man's Desiring," and many more. Pages are cross-referenced for supplements.
00699020 Book $5.95
00697313 Book/CD Pack..$9.95

HAL LEONARD METHOD BOOK 3

Book 3 includes the chromatic scale, 16th notes, playing in 2nd, 4th, 5th and 7th positions, moving chords up the neck (bar chords), finger picking, ensembles and solos, a wide variety of style studies and many excellent songs for playing and/or singing. Can be used with supplements.
00699030 Book $5.95
00697316 Book/CD Pack........................$9.95

COMPOSITE

Books 1, 2, and 3 bound together in an easy-to-use spiral binding.
00699040 ....$14.95

GUITAR METHOD SUPPLEMENTS

Hal Leonard Pop Melody Supplements are the unique books that supplement any guitar method books 1, 2, or 3. The play-along audio features guitar on the left channel and full rhythm section on the right. Each book is filled with great pop songs that students are eager to play! Now available in book/CD packs!

EASY POP MELODIES

A unique pop supplement to any guitar method book 1. Cross-referenced with Hal Leonard Guitar Method Book 1 pages for easy student and teacher use. Featured songs: "Feelings," "Let It Be," "Every Breath You Take," "You Needed Me" and "Heartbreak Hotel."

00697281 Book....................................$5.95
00699148 Book/Cassette Pack...........................$12.95
00697268 Book/CD Pack $14.95

MORE EASY POP MELODIES

A unique pop supplement to any guitar method book 2. Cross-referenced with Hal Leonard Guitar Method Book 2 pages for easy student and teacher use. Featured songs: "Long and Winding Road," "Say, Say, Say," "King of Pain," and more.

00697280 Book....................................$5.95
00699149 Book/Cassette Pack...........................$12.95
00697269 Book/CD Pack $14.95

POP MELODIES PLUS

Pop supplement to Book 3. Pop Melodies Plus features "Cool Change," "Daniel," "Don't Be Cruel," "Memory," "Maneater" and many more. 14 songs in all.

00699154 Book....................................$5.95
00697270 Book/CD Pack...........................$14.95

FOR MORE INFORMATION, SEE YOUR LOCAL MUSIC DEALER, OR WRITE TO:

HAL•LEONARD® CORPORATION
7777 W. BLUEMOUND RD. P.O. BOX 13819 MILWAUKEE, WI 53213

http://www.halleonard.com

Prices, contents and availability subject to change without notice.

ROCK TRAX 1

Rock Trax is a supplement to any method book 1. It also teaches rhythm guitar, lead guitar and solo licks. The exciting play-along audio features a great-sounding rhythm section and demonstrates each exercise in the book. Rock Trax is unique because it provides the teacher with a program to teach rock guitar technique when the student begins lessons.
00699165 Book/Cassette Pack $12.95
00697271 Book/CD Pack.....................................$14.95

ROCK TRAX 2

This rock guitar supplement to any method book 2 teaches rhythm guitar, lead improvisation and solo licks. The tape provides eight background rhythm tracks and demonstrates both the solo licks and new rock guitar techniques.

00697272 Book/CD Pack.....................................$14.95

ROCK HITS FOR 1, 2, OR 3 GUITARS

Supplement to any method books 1 and 2. These arrangements are playable by 1, 2, or 3 guitars or class/ensemble. The audio features lead, harmony, and rhythm guitar parts with band backup on side A. Side B repeats the complete band accompaniments without guitar parts 1 or 2. "Practice notes" give the student additional playing tips. Contents: Sister Christian • Rock Around The Clock • Johnny B. Goode • Rocket Man • Sad Songs (Say So Much) • Hungry Like The Wolf • Maggie May.
00699168 Book/Cassette Pack $12.95
00697273 Book/CD Pack.....................................$14.95

INCREDIBLE CHORD FINDER

A complete guide diagramming over 1,000 guitar chords in their most common voicings. The book is arranged chromatically and each chord is illustrated in three ways for three levels of difficulty: the easiest form of the chords for the beginner and the more difficult versions for the intermediate and advanced players. Note names of each string are indicated on each chord diagram to let the player know what notes are being played in the chord.
00697200 6" x 9" $4.95
00697208 9" x 12" $5.95

RHYTHM GUITAR PLAY-ALONG

Strum along with your favorite hits from The Beatles, the Rolling Stones, the Eagles, Eric Clapton, and more! The songs are presented in order of difficulty – beginning with simple three- and four-note tunes and ending with songs that contain many chords, including seventh chords and barre chords. The accompanying CD features each song recorded by a full band, so you can hear how each song sounds and then play along when you're ready. 20 songs in all: Angie • Brown Eyed Girl • Dreams • Evil Ways • Free Bird • Twist and Shout • Wild Thing • Wonderful Tonight • more. This book is intended as a supplement to the Hal Leonard Guitar Method but can also be used with any beginning guitar method.
00697309 Book/CD Pack.....................................$12.95

0200